A Discovery Biography

Harry S. Truman

—◆—

People's President

by David R. Collins
illustrated by Paul Frame

CHELSEA JUNIORS
A division of Chelsea House Publishers
New York ◆ Philadelphia

BB

This book is for my mother, whose love, strength, and
encouragement exceed human measurement.

The Discovery Books have been prepared under the
educational supervision of Mary C. Austin, Ed.D.,
Reading Specialist and Professor of Education, Case
Western Reserve University.

Cover illustration: Janet Hamlin

First Chelsea House edition 1991

1 3 5 7 9 8 6 4 2

ISBN 0-7910-1421-5

90-35485

Contents

Chapter *1*

A Special Day

Eight-year-old Harry Truman sat up in his bed. He listened closely. Strange noises were coming from the roof overhead.

"Vivian! Wake up!" Harry whispered to his brother across the room.

"What is it?" Vivian asked, sitting up and rubbing his eyes.

Harry reached for his glasses on the table beside his bed. He ran to the window and opened it wide. Six-year-old Vivian followed.

It was a warm November morning in the year 1892. Most people in the town of Independence, Missouri, were still asleep.

"Listen!" Harry exclaimed. "There's someone on the roof!"

"What should we do?" said Vivian.

Harry thought a moment. Then he leaned out the window.

"Who's on our roof?" Harry called in a low, gruff voice.

"It's a foolish boy who does not know his own father!" came the answer. "Get washed and dressed. Come out into the front yard."

Minutes later Harry and Vivian ran into the yard. They looked up at the flag flying on top of the roof.

"It's a special day, boys," Mr. Truman called. "We just got news that Cleveland won the election. He's our new president!"

"Hooray!" the two boys cheered.

"He won because you worked so hard to get votes for him!" Harry cried.

Mr. Truman laughed. "Well, you both get started with your chores. I'll have a surprise for you tonight."

Harry pulled his brother's arm. "Let's hurry, Vivian. We've got a lot of work to do."

There was always "work to do" around the Truman house. John Truman, Harry's father, was an animal trader. He kept farm animals in his seven acre backyard.

Early each morning Harry headed for the barn. First he milked the cows. Then he fed the mules and horses. Vivian gathered the eggs from the hen house. Together the boys walked the goats to the public spring for drinking water.

There would be time for play after lunch. But Harry always looked forward to late afternoon when Mrs. Truman read aloud to the boys. Even two-year-old Mary Jane Truman was quiet as her mother read.

Harry and Vivian also took turns reading. Harry liked stories about people in history.

"Are there any more books about generals?" he asked. "Can we read another story about George Washington?"

"We'll start one tomorrow," Mrs. Truman said.

That night Mr. Truman did not come home for supper. The boys were worried. "Maybe he forgot the surprise he told us about," said Harry.

Mrs. Truman shook her head. "The surprise will be at the town square. We're to be there at eight o'clock.

Harry, you can wear your election cap."

Harry dashed upstairs and got the cap. Mr. Truman had given it to him weeks ago. The writing on the white cap said "Cleveland for President."

When they were ready, Mrs. Truman and her children went to the town square. It seemed as if everyone in Independence were there. People were singing and laughing. Firecrackers popped. Bright torches were lighted. A big sign said: Victory for Cleveland.

A drummer pounded a drum. A band started to play. A parade marched around the town square.

Suddenly Harry saw his father riding a tall gray horse.

"We won!" Harry shouted as Mr. Truman rode by. Young Harry waved his cap in the air. "We won!"

Chapter *2*

The Waldo Street Gang

When Harry was twelve years old, the Truman family moved to a house on Waldo Street in Independence. Boys and girls in the neighborhood were called the "Waldo Street Gang."

Harry liked his new friends. They often played at a nearby pond. During the summer they went swimming. In winter, they skated on the ice.

Sometimes the gang played baseball. Harry was not allowed to play because he wore glasses and might break them in rough play. So the gang asked him to umpire.

One girl in the group could do everything well. Her name was Elizabeth Wallace. Her friends called her "Bess."

Harry liked to watch Bess Wallace. She skated faster than anyone, and she always hit home runs.

One day Harry walked home from school with Bess. "I wish I could play baseball like you," he said.

Bess just smiled. "I wish I knew as much about history as you do."

Harry did know a lot about history. He spent much of his time reading. Once he was sick and had to stay out of school for months. He did his schoolwork at home. Mrs. Truman always took time to hear Harry's lessons. When he returned to class, Harry was far ahead of his classmates!

Harry was ten when he began taking piano lessons. At first his mother taught him. But soon he played so well Mrs. Truman sent him to another teacher.

One afternoon Harry was running down the street. He was on his way to his piano lesson.

"Hey, Harry!" came a shout from behind.

Harry stopped and turned around. Four boys from the neighborhood came running up to him.

"We're going fishing down at the river," one of the boys said. "Come with us."

Harry thought a moment. It *would* be fun to go fishing.

But Harry knew his parents had to pay for his lessons. Besides, he liked playing the piano. That was fun too.

"No," Harry answered. "I've got to take my lesson."

The boys turned and walked away. They began singing a song Harry had heard many times before.

Harry T. can't come and play
Harry's playing his piano today...

Harry stood with his fists clenched. He did not like being teased. But he was not going to let a little teasing change his mind. Quickly he hurried on to his lesson.

All through grammar school Harry spent his spare time reading and playing the piano. When he got to high school, he was still interested in books and music, but he decided he wanted to earn some money too. He got a job at a drugstore.

Each day Harry went to the drugstore at 6:30 in the morning. He swept and mopped the floors. Then he washed the windows and dusted the display cases. He worked fast and watched the clock so he wouldn't be late for school. Harry was paid three dollars a week.

The Democratic National Convention of 1900 was going to be held in nearby Kansas City. People from all over the country would gather to choose a man to run for the highest office—the presidency of the United States. Mr. Truman planned to go to the convention. Harry wanted to go too.

He got his wish. Mr. Truman told him that a sixteen-year-old boy could be useful there. In July Mr. Truman and Harry left for Kansas City.

Seventeen thousand people filled the new Convention Hall. Harry had never seen so many people. It was a busy,

noisy place. Bands played. People talked and laughed. Men stood on a flag-draped platform shouting speeches to the crowd.

Mr. Truman listened to thc speeches while Harry ran errands.

Those in charge shouted to him.

"Here, boy, set up a row of seats back here."

"Take this note over to the people in the New York section."

Harry had little time for rest. But the work was fun. Harry felt he was a part of history being made.

When he returned to Independence, Harry told his friends about the convention. In the fall he wrote about it in the school newspaper.

It was not long before Harry would be graduated from high school. He began to think about his future. For years he had dreamed of becoming a great general. He wanted to attend the U.S. Military Academy at West Point.

Harry was graduated from Independence High School in 1901. That summer he studied hard for the West Point entrance tests.

But Harry never took them. He found out that he would not be able to pass the medical examination. His eyesight was too poor.

Harry felt defeated. "I don't know what to do now," he told his father.

"It will work out all right," Mr. Truman answered. "Just keep looking until you find the right door. When you find it, go in."

Harry thought about his father's words. "Find the right door . . . go in."

Harry was eager to find the right door.

Chapter *3*

Sounds of War

Soon after his graduation, Harry was needed to help Vivian and Mary Jane finish high school. Mr. Truman had invested money in the grain market. The market failed and the money was lost.

Harry took a job working on a railroad. One morning he stood on a railroad handcar. Up and down he pumped the handle to make the handcar roll along the track. The sun was hot. Harry wiped his face with his sleeve.

"That's mighty hard work, young fella!" another worker called to Harry. "You had better stop for a rest."

Harry shook his head. "Rest comes after my work gets done," he shouted.

Twice a day Harry pumped his handcar to three different railroad camps. He kept the time records for four hundred men who laid track for the railroad. The camps where the men lived while they worked were like tiny towns. Harry made many friends in them.

When Vivian graduated from high school, the two Truman sons decided to find jobs in the same bank. Harry soon grew tired of the job.

"I don't have enough work to do," he told his father at breakfast one day. "Someone tells me what to do. I want to make my own decisions."

"I'm going to help your Grandma Young run her farm," Mr. Truman said. "We need an extra worker. I could use you there."

Harry liked the idea. He gave up his bank job and went to the farm.

Harry got up at 4:30 each morning. He milked cows, fed the hogs, and pitched hay. He helped his father in the fields too.

On hot, sunny days, Mrs. Truman drove the buggy out to the fields. She brought cool lemonade. One afternoon she called to Harry, "Stop your work for a little while. Come drink some lemonade."

As Harry drank, his mother stood up in the buggy. She looked at the long rows.

"You plant a good straight row of corn, son."

Harry laughed at that. "If I didn't, dad would sure make me plant them all over again."

Harry liked working on the farm. Even after his father died, Harry stayed on there. Often he rode into Independence to visit Bess Wallace. They went on picnics and to concerts together. They talked about getting married someday.

When the United States entered World War I in 1917, Harry put aside marriage plans. Men were needed to fight. Harry was among the first to sign up. In spite of his weak eyesight, he was accepted.

"Will you wait for me?" Harry asked Bess.

Harry did not have to ask. He knew Bess cared only for him.

Harry missed Bess, but life in an

army training camp was an exciting, new experience. At that time soldiers could choose their own officers. Many soldiers liked Harry. They elected him their lieutenant. At age 33, Lieutenant Harry Truman went overseas. In France he was promoted to captain and led two hundred men.

The unit Harry commanded was called Battery D. While training in France, some of the soldiers decided to test Harry. They wanted to know if their officer would be calm and brave in the face of danger.

Battery D had 160 horses in the unit. The horses were used mostly to pull the four big guns of the battery. One night the men turned all the horses loose.

"It's a stampede!" one man yelled. "The horses are loose!"

Harry ran out of his tent. Since he had grown up around horses, he knew it was not a real stampede. He knew that the men were playing a trick on him.

Harry was calm. He watched the horses quietly for a while. Then he walked over to the men.

"Looks like you had better get to work," Harry said. "These horses have to be rounded up."

As Harry walked away, one of the men laughed. "That captain of ours wasn't scared at all!"

For months Harry and his men trained for battle. Finally they were sent to fight the enemy soldiers.

Some of Harry's men were frightened. Harry ran forward, shouting orders. "Forward! Move forward! Come on, men, move! Forward!"

Harry was a good leader. His strong words helped his men win many battles.

Harry soon became a "spotter" where battles were being fought. As a spotter, he moved ahead of other soldiers. When he spotted the enemy, he used his field phone. Harry called his commanding officers to tell them what the enemy was doing.

One night Harry and his men camped near an orchard. Enemy soldiers were camped nearby. Harry had received orders not to fire on the enemy unless they attacked first.

Harry crawled ahead to see what the enemy was doing. He saw they were moving quickly out of camp. They were moving toward another American camp.

"I've got to do something!" Harry told himself.

There was no time to call his commanding officers. Still, he had orders not to fire on the enemy. Orders or no orders, action was needed. Quickly Harry got back to his men.

"German soldiers are advancing to the right!" Harry called out. "Open fire!"

Harry's men began to shoot. The German soldiers were startled. They had not expected an attack. They ran back to their camp.

"Your brave action saved many lives," another officer told Harry. "That was a good decision. I'm glad you had the courage to make it alone."

In November 1918, World War I ended. Captain Harry Truman and his men remained overseas until April 1919.

Harry was happy when he boarded a ship for America. He knew Bess was waiting for him in Independence. Each of her letters reminded Harry of her promise to wait for him. But their future together was uncertain. How would Harry earn a living? He had found that men liked and trusted him. They were willing to follow him, and he enjoyed being a leader. Yes, maybe liking people and wanting to work with them was a clue to the "right door" . . .

Chapter 4

Open for Business

The day was June 28, 1919. Harry and Bess stood before the altar of a church in Independence. When he heard the words, "I now pronounce you man and wife," Harry beamed with happiness.

Harry and Bess took a short wedding trip. When they returned to Independence, they moved into a big house with Bess's mother and grandmother.

Harry knew that he did not want to go back to farming. He had enjoyed working on the farm, but now he wanted to try something else. He started to look for a job. In nearby Kansas City, Harry had lunch with an old friend, Eddie Jacobson. Eddie had an idea.

"I sold shirts before the war," Eddie said. "I was pretty good at it. But now I'd like to do something else."

Harry nodded. "I'm looking for something else to do too. I want Bess to have more than I could give her as a farmer."

"Well, I know quite a bit about men's clothes." Eddie rubbed his chin thoughtfully. "Maybe we could work together. We could open a clothing store for men."

Harry liked Eddie's idea. The two men decided to become partners.

Money was needed to open the

business. Harry sold his share of his grandmother's farm.

In November 1919, a new store opened in Kansas City. Harry climbed a ladder and hung a big sign above the door.

TRUMAN & JACOBSON

MEN'S CLOTHING

OPEN FOR BUSINESS

Business was good at the Truman and Jacobson store. Often Harry's old soldier friends came by. He took care of the store records and books. Eddie ordered the clothing that was to be sold. Both men worked as clerks.

Harry worked six days a week. Each morning he opened the store at eight o'clock. After closing it at nine each night, he checked the day's sales.

In 1922 a great depression hit the country. Businesses failed. Men lost their jobs. Fewer customers came into Truman and Jacobson's store.

Soon not enough money was coming in to pay the bills. The men knew they must close the store. They were in debt.

Harry felt like a failure. Bess tried to comfort him. "Lots of good people owe money now, Harry," she said. "Everyone trusts you. They know you will pay them when you can."

Harry had time now to give new thought to his future. He was sure of one thing. He enjoyed working with people. Maybe he ought to go into politics. One day Jim Pendergast, an officer Harry had known during the war, came into the store.

"Jim, I think I'd like to run for the

job of county judge," Harry said. "Your family knows a lot about the political system here in Missouri. Do you think they'd talk to me about it?"

"You've sure got a lot of friends around here," Jim answered. "I think you'd make a good candidate for the office. I'll tell my father about you."

"I don't have any law training," Harry added. "All I know is I like working with people and trying to help them."

Jim smiled. "The law training can come later. First you've got to want to work hard for the people."

"That much I am sure of," Harry answered.

Chapter *5*

First Election

Soon after Jim and Harry's talk, Jim's father, Mike Pendergast, came to see Harry.

Mike Pendergast and his brother Tom knew a great deal about politics in Missouri. Some people called the two brothers "political bosses."

"So you want to run for county judge," Mike Pendergast said. "Well, I think we can help you. Maybe you can help us a little too."

After his talk with Mike Pendergast, Harry talked with Bess.

"I know I need the Pendergasts to

help me win. I only hope they don't expect me to take orders from them if I'm elected."

Bess smiled. "If they had asked me, I could have told them that it would be easier to give orders to a Missouri mule," she teased. "But they'll find out soon enough."

Harry knew the duties of county judge. He did not work in a law court. The county judge helped set taxes and plan new roads. He helped get bridges built.

To win the election, Harry knew he had to visit the voters. He bought an old car and drove all over the county. He spoke at picnics and club meetings.

"I want to work for you!" Harry shouted from atop a picnic table one afternoon. "You vote for *me* and I'll work for *you*!"

Some businessmen wanted to make deals with Harry.

"Will you get me the job of building new bridges if I help you?" one man asked.

"I'll have my workmen vote for you," promised another man. "But only if you let us build all the new roads."

Harry refused to make any deals.

"County jobs will go to the companies that do the best work for the least money. That's the only promise I'll make."

Harry tried to visit every town in the county. He talked to people in stores and on street corners. He listened to people and their ideas.

"Most fellows running for election like to do all the talking," said one farmer. "I like this Harry Truman. He listens too. He's got my vote."

Many others felt the same way. When the election votes were counted, Harry was happy. He had won his first election.

As county judge, Harry continued to drive around and visit people. He watched the workmen at their jobs. He knocked on people's front doors.

"I'm Harry Truman, your county judge," he would say. "I just thought I'd stop by for a minute and visit."

At the same time, Harry studied law at night. He thought that a knowledge of law would help him do a better job.

On February 17, 1924, Bess Truman gave birth to a baby girl. Bess and Harry had been very excited about becoming parents. They were so excited before the baby came that they forgot to get a crib.

"Harry, you'll have to find a crib in a hurry," Bess laughed. "Mary Margaret needs a warm bed."

Harry thought a moment. Then he walked over to the bedroom dresser. He pulled one drawer out halfway and took his clothes out of it.

"Let's use this," Harry suggested. "With a little soft padding, this will make a fine bed."

Harry was right. The "dresser bed" was safe and warm.

A few months later Harry ran for election again. Since he had refused to take orders from some men, Harry had made enemies. These men worked hard to beat Harry. In the 1924 election Harry was defeated.

So he returned to banking. But he did not forget the county judge's job. In two years Harry decided to run again. This time he ran for the job of presiding judge, a county job with more responsibility. He won easily.

For the next eight years Harry worked hard for the county. He saw to it that better roads were built. New playgrounds and parks were opened. A new hospital and a new police building were built. People trusted Harry and voted for him.

Harry liked being presiding judge. But he thought he could do more for the people in Washington. In 1934 Harry made a big decision.

"I'm going to run for the United States Senate," he said one night.

Bess nodded her agreement. "And if you're elected, you'll be a fine senator."

"I'd vote for you, daddy!" Mary Margaret said. "I would if I could!"

44

Chapter 6

Through Senate Doors

Harry stood on a platform under the hot July sun. He looked over the crowd of people in front of him. Bess sat in the front row of seats. Ten-year-old Margaret wiggled beside her.

"I'm glad to be here," Harry told the people. "I should be tired since this is my sixth speech today. But talking to people gives me pep. I hope you'll give me the chance to take that pep to Washington, D.C."

The crowd laughed and clapped. People liked to hear Harry talk. He never used fancy words. He talked about food prices and farming. Harry knew what people wanted and needed.

Harry spent the summer of 1934 giving speeches. Day after day he met new crowds of people. Harry liked to have Bess and Margaret with him.

The battle for the senator's office was long and tiring. Tom Pendergast gave Harry advice. Mike had died a few years before.

Finally election day came. When the votes were counted, Harry was declared the winner.

Harry's friends in Independence gave him a victory party. One woman stood up and gave a surprising speech.

"Someday you're going to be the president of the United States!" The woman smiled. "Then we'll give you another victory party."

Harry laughed at this friendly nonsense.

When he got to Washington, Harry looked for a new home. He found an apartment and sent for Bess and Margaret.

Not everyone was friendly to Harry in Washington, D.C. Some people did not think Tom Pendergast was honest. Since he had helped Harry, maybe Harry was taking orders from him. People didn't trust a senator who was run by a boss.

"I've got to show people I make my own decisions," Harry told Bess. "I've got to prove I'm not just an errand boy."

Harry worked hard. His desk was always stacked high with papers. Each day he went to committee meetings. He became interested in the country's railroads. He worked hard at the railroad committee meetings.

"We all know many railroad tracks are in poor condition." Harry looked at the other committee members seated at the table. "People should be able to ride in safety. Let's not talk about the problem any longer. Let's do something. Let's get these tracks fixed."

Railroad officers listened to Harry's ideas. Soon new tracks were laid. New stations were built.

Harry liked being a senator. But he liked the times he could relax too. The best times were evenings at home.

"How about some piano music?" Harry would ask Margaret.

Margaret always jumped up quickly. She loved playing the piano. Often she sang as she played.

"Now, you play," Margaret would say to her father. "Let's play some songs together."

Harry seldom refused. He enjoyed playing the piano. It reminded him of home in Independence.

As a senator Harry learned about many problems in the world. More and more news came of troubles overseas. Germany, Italy, and Japan had formed big armies. Soldiers from these countries were attacking other countries.

In December 1941, Japan attacked a United States base in Pearl Harbor, Hawaii. Americans were stunned and shocked. President Roosevelt asked Congress to declare war.

"We have no choice," Harry told his friends. "I only hope it will not last long."

Chapter 7

Into the White House

Harry sat at a long table. He was chairman of a committee to investigate the defense program. For a long time Harry listened to the other senators at the table. Then he took his turn.

"Our committee has met many times," Harry said. "We know that a lot of defense money has been wasted. It's up to us to stop this waste. The lives of our soldiers depend on us. The future of our country depends on what we do."

News about Harry's committee filled the newspapers. People across the

country read about Senator Truman's work. President Franklin Roosevelt liked the work Harry was doing. One afternoon the president invited Harry to the White House.

Harry felt a bit uneasy about this invitation. They had talked before, but this was the first time he had been called alone to the president's office.

"President Roosevelt is the busiest and most powerful man in the world," Harry told Bess. "I'm surprised that he's taking time to talk with me."

Bess shook her head and straightened Harry's tie. "I think it shows how wise the president is. He takes time to talk to his best helpers."

When Harry entered the president's office, he still felt uneasy. Mr. Roosevelt sat behind a big desk. He looked up and smiled.

"Have a seat," the president said. "I just wanted you to know your country is grateful for your work. Wars are not always won on the battlefields. We need soldiers like you too."

President Roosevelt's praise pleased Harry. He promised himself to work even harder. In the months ahead he found more ways to save money. Now more money could be spent building ships and airplanes to win the war.

In 1944 the Democrats met in Chicago to pick men to run for president and vice-president. President Roosevelt decided to run for reelection. Many party leaders wanted Harry to run with him for vice-president.

"I like being a senator," Harry told Bess. "It's a tough job, but it's work I like doing. I hope the party and

President Roosevelt will choose someone else."

But Democratic leaders decided Truman was the best man for the job. As Harry sat in a Chicago hotel room, President Roosevelt called. He said he too wanted Harry to run for vice-president.

Harry felt it was his duty to accept.

President Roosevelt gave few speeches during the campaign. He was busy with the war and not in good health. Harry went from city to city giving hundreds of speeches.

In November, the newspapers ran big headlines.

ROOSEVELT, TRUMAN ELECTED!

As vice-president, Harry was the main officer in the Senate. He liked that part of the job. But President Roosevelt was busy running the war and meeting with leaders of other countries. He had no time to let Harry know all that was going on. Harry did his best to learn by himself.

Then, one day, Harry received an urgent call: "Come to the White House at once." Harry was uneasy for he did not know what to expect.

When Harry arrived, Mrs. Roosevelt was waiting for him.

"Harry, the president is dead," she said gently.

President Roosevelt dead? Harry could not believe it. But Mrs. Roosevelt's face told him it was true.

"Is there anything I can do for you?" Harry asked, his voice trembling.

Mrs. Roosevelt shook her head. "Is

there anything *we* can do for you? You are the one in trouble now."

Mrs. Roosevelt was right. Harry had been vice-president for only 82 days, and suddenly he was president of the United States. Harry was overwhelmed. America was still at war. People trusted Roosevelt to win the war and find peace. Harry was not well known. He knew people would fear he could not do the job. Still the lives of thousands, and perhaps the future of the country, now depended on Harry's decisions. He had a job to do.

Harry spoke to the American people on the radio.

"I shall do my best," Harry promised. "I shall work to end the war quickly. But I cannot do this job alone. All the people in this country must help me."

Chapter **8**

Big Decisions

Harry S. Truman became president of the United States on April 12, 1945. Less than a month later, on his 61st birthday, he received good news from Europe.

"The fighting in Europe is over," President Truman announced. "Let us now work even harder for peace."

The new president led the way. In June of 1945 he went to San Francisco. He joined people from all over the world who had come to form a new organization—the United

Nations. Truman spoke for the United States.

"Once this war is over, we must be ready to work together to stop all wars. We must build a world of peace."

After speaking in San Francisco, President Truman went to other meetings. He talked to the leaders of the countries who were friends of the United States. The big question was how to get Japan to stop fighting.

One afternoon President Truman met with American scientists and generals. They talked about a big bomb the United States had built and tested. The bomb used atomic energy and was called the atom bomb.

"No other country has such a weapon," one of the scientists said. "The atom bomb can destroy cities."

One of the generals spoke up. "The Japanese army and navy are still strong. If we attack Japan by ship and plane, we will lose thousands of our fighting men."

President Truman thought a long time about the bomb. Again and again he talked to generals and scientists. Finally, he made up his mind.

In August 1945, two atom bombs were dropped on Japan. Two large cities were destroyed. Thousands of people were killed. The leaders of Japan knew they could not fight back against such weapons. Soon the war came to an end. But some people said the United States was wrong to use the atom bomb.

The president stuck by his decision. "War is terrible," he said. "I wanted to end the fighting as fast as possible. If some people want to blame me for using the bomb, let them. But the war is over. Now we can start working together—for peace."

The work started at once. People in Europe were starving. President Truman, acting for the people of America, sent food. He also sent money to help rebuild homes, factories, and businesses.

"America will always help countries that need help," said Truman. "We stand ready to assist and support, but never to dictate."

Slowly the war-torn countries regained strength. President Truman opened new trade markets and signed new peace plans.

In the United States, President Truman faced new problems too.

Business leaders and working men did not agree over wages. Farmers wanted higher prices for their crops. Again, President Truman took charge. He suggested new ways of handling the problems. His suggestions later became known as the "Fair Deal" program.

Every day there was work to be done. There was always one more important person to talk to the president.

Truman knew he had to stay healthy to carry out his duties. Each morning he took a two mile walk. His bodyguards and news reporters went with him. But they could not always keep up with his brisk pace.

"You boys better start getting in shape," Truman teased. "Or maybe you could borrow some bicycles."

During one morning walk, Truman

crossed the bridge over the Potomac River. On the bridge he passed an open door. The president went in.

Truman's guards did not see where he went. Quickly they searched the bridge. They found the president talking to a bridge worker.

"Mr. President!" one of the guards said. "We've been looking all over for you!"

President Truman smiled. "I've just been visiting with this fellow. He has some good ideas about the country."

"But there are people waiting to see you at the White House."

Harry Truman stood up. "I don't think I should listen only to people who come to see me. I've got to get out and talk to other people. Some people are too busy to come and see me."

Too busy to come and see the president? Harry Truman's bodyguards laughed. But they knew he meant what he said.

A presidential election was to be held in 1948. President Truman knew he faced a battle if he wanted to be president again. Many business leaders did not like his programs.

Truman thought his programs would work. He believed that if he could explain them to the people, they would agree with him. President Truman decided to run for election.

For weeks and weeks Harry Truman rode in a train across the country. He spoke to the crowds from the back of his "Truman Train." Often Bess and Margaret went along. He always wanted them to say hello to the people.

"I want you to meet the boss," President Truman would say as Bess stepped forward. "And I want you to meet the boss's boss too," he would add, as Margaret joined her parents.

Most people said Truman could not win. President Truman knew the vote would be close, but he wasn't worried. On election night people stayed up late to learn who had won. But Harry Truman went to bed early. Around 3 A.M., a friend awoke him. He had won the election.

Harry Truman began four more years in the White House.

Chapter **9**

Peace and War

The table at the White House was set for breakfast. Harry Truman sat down and picked up a newspaper.

Suddenly the floor shook. The dishes on the table rattled.

"What was that?" Bess asked.

The president shook his head. "I'm afraid this place needs some fixing up. It's 150 years old."

Painters and builders were called in. The president and his family moved out while the White House was done over. New boards and beams made the floors stronger. Fresh paint covered the walls. Finally, the work was finished. The Trumans were happy to return to the White House.

It was easy to do over the White House. It was more difficult to solve the country's other problems. Hour after hour Truman worked at his desk. He met visitors and gave speeches.

The president's doctors told him to slow down. He was 65 years old now. Often he worked sixteen hours a day.

In 1950 trouble came to a small country across the sea. The country of Korea was divided into two parts, north and south. The northern part of Korea was run by Communists. Slowly Communist soldiers moved into the southern part. The leaders of South Korea asked the United States to help push the Communist soldiers out.

President Truman acted quickly. He asked the United Nations to help stop the North Koreans. He appointed General Douglas MacArthur to be the commander of American troops being sent to Korea. He hoped the problems would soon end.

Weeks became months. Still the fighting continued. More and more American soldiers were being killed. Some people felt the United States should withdraw from the fighting.

"We're fighting in Korea because we care about freedom," Truman said. "A country is more than land and buildings. A country is also people. Americans have always cared about people. We must help people stay free."

Not everyone agreed with President Truman. Some people thought it was foolish to be fighting in a country so far away. General MacArthur did not agree with the president in another way. When China sent soldiers to help North Korea, MacArthur thought the Americans should attack Chinese bases. He began to ignore the president's orders and told newspaper reporters Truman was making a mistake.

But President Truman was the commander in chief. He could not have a general disobeying orders. He took away MacArthur's command and brought him back to the United States. Many people admired General MacArthur. They said Harry Truman was wrong and foolish.

Truman stood firm. "A president must make his decisions and stick with them. Some people may call him

a fool. That's all right. If you can't stand the heat, you should get out of the kitchen. I can stand the heat."

The fighting was still going on in 1952. Harry Truman faced another big decision. Should he run for president again? His friends told him he should.

"You've done a great job, Harry," one of them said. "No one could have done a finer job of helping countries after President Roosevelt died. The country needs another four years with Truman."

President Truman thought it over. Then he made a short announcement.

"I have served my country for a long time. I have tried to serve it well. I shall not run for reelection."

Letters came in from all over the country. People from every state urged Truman to run for president again.

"We believe in you," wrote a group of farmers in Iowa. "We know you will keep your promises."

"You are honest and we trust you," wrote a church club in California. "We hope you'll change your mind."

A first grade class in Florida also wrote President Truman: "You are a good man. Do not leave the White House. Stay there. Please."

Harry read the letters. They made him feel happy and proud. But he stood firm in his decision.

In January 1953 Harry and Bess boarded a train. A big crowd stood in the Washington railroad station. People had come to say good-bye.

Smiling and cheerful, Harry waved to the people. Slowly the train pulled out of the station.

Harry S. Truman was going home.

Chapter *10*

"Just Call Me Harry"

It was a warm spring morning in Independence. Shop owners in the town began opening their stores. Most of the streets were still empty.

But Harry Truman was up for an early morning walk. He tapped his cane lightly as he strolled. Often he stopped to greet his friends.

"A good morning to you, Bill. How is everything with your barbershop?"

"Just fine, Mr. President."

Harry smiled and shook his head. "It's not Mr. President anymore, Bill. Just call me Harry. I'm nobody special."

Harry was wrong. To the people of Independence, Harry was "Mr. Citizen." He was someone special to thousands of other people too. Each day Harry received piles of letters. People wrote to thank him for his work as president.

Harry kept busy. He wrote books about his life in the White House.

He helped make plans for a new library in Independence. The library would keep Mr. Truman's many important papers and letters.

Whenever he could, Harry took trips with Bess. Sometimes he was given awards and honors. But Harry enjoyed meeting new people most. On one trip a filling station man came running out to Harry's car.

"Golly, Mister, you sure look a lot like Harry Truman!" the man said.

Harry laughed. "Well, I guess I should!"

In 1956 a big wedding was held in Independence. Margaret Truman married Clifton Daniel from New York. Harry proudly walked beside his only daughter up the church aisle.

"She was a beautiful bride," Bess told Harry after the wedding.

"Just like her mother was!" Harry answered.

In 1957 the Harry S. Truman Library opened. Each day Harry walked from his home to his new office in the building. Often he spoke to groups of boys and girls who came to the library.

"The story of America is as exciting as any story you'll ever read," he said. "If you know your country's history, you will be proud to be an American."

Harry kept up his interest in politics. Men who were running for office came to him for advice. He liked going to the conventions and giving speeches.

But time was passing by. Harry's steps became slower. Illness often kept him inside his Independence home.

In the fall of 1972 people learned Harry was very sick. Still Harry fought back.

"He may be 88 years old," said one doctor, "but he fights like a man of 20."

It was a fight Harry could not win. He died on December 26, 1972.

People all over the world were sad to hear the news. President Nixon and other famous people flew to Independence. Thousands of people came to the funeral. Harry was buried near the library he loved.

"Harry S. Truman knew great people and did great things," wrote one newspaper reporter. "He did what he thought best for people, all people. He'll always be remembered as the people's president."